P9-BYJ-782

WITHDRAWN

DEMCO

Dinosaurs Alive!

Pteranodon

and Other Flying Reptiles

Jinny Johnson

Illustrated by Graham Rosewarne

A^+

Smart Apple Media

Smart Apple Media is published by Black Rabbit Books
P.O. Box 3263, Mankato, Minnesota 56002

Designed by Helen James
Edited by Mary-Jane Wilkins
Artwork by Graham Rosewarne

Photograph on page 28 by Lawrence Lawry / Science Photo Library

Printed in the United States

Library of Congress Cataloging-in-Publication Data

Johnson, Jinny.
Pteranodon and other flying reptiles / by Jinny Johnson.
p. cm. – (Dinosaurs alive!)
Includes index.
ISBN 978-1-59920-068-2
1. Pterosauria—Juvenile literature. 2. Pteranodon—Juvenile literature. I.
Title.

QE862.P7J65 2007
567.918—dc22   2007009894

9 8 7 6 5 4 3 2

Contents

A pterosaur's world

The pterosaurs were not dinosaurs. They were flying reptiles that lived long ago, at the same time as dinosaurs. Pterosaur means "winged lizard."

The first pterosaurs lived about 215 million years ago, before there were any bats or birds. They ruled the skies for more than 150 million years until they disappeared—became extinct—about 65 million years ago.

Some pterosaurs were no bigger than a bird, such as a robin, but others were the size of a small airplane. There were two main groups of pterosaurs. The first to exist were the long-tailed rhamphorhynchoids, and later, the short-tailed pterodactyloids.

Dsungaripterus

TRIASSIC
248 to 205 million years ago
Some creatures that lived at this time:
Eudimorphodon Coelophysis, Eoraptor,
Liliensternus, Plateosaurus, Riojasaurus

EARLY JURASSIC
205 to 180 million years ago
Some creatures that lived at this time:
Dimorphodon Crylophosaurus, Dilophosaurus,
Lesothosaurus, Massospondylus, Scelidosaurus

Dimorphodon

LATE JURASSIC
180 to 144 million years ago
Some creatures that lived at this time:
Rhamphorhynchus, Allosaurus, Apatosaurus,
Brachiosaurus, Ornitholestes, Stegosaurus

EARLY CRETACEOUS
144 to 98 million years ago
Some creatures that lived at this time:
Pterodaustro, Baryonyx, Giganotosaurus, Iguanodon,
Leaellynasaura, Muttaburrasaurus, Nodosaurus

LATE CRETACEOUS
98 to 65 million years ago
Some creatures that lived at this time:
Pteranodon, Ankylosaurus, Gallimimus, Maiasaura,
Triceratops, Tyrannosaurus

Pteranodon

Pteranodon

This amazing pterosaur was one of the biggest. Its wings were enormous and it had a huge head that, from beak to crest, was longer than an adult human.

All pterosaurs had big brains for their size, and they were probably more intelligent than reptiles are today. They also had very good eyesight and hearing. Many dinosaur experts think that pterosaurs were covered with hair or fur to keep them warm.

The pteranodon's long beak was toothless, but many other pterosaurs had teeth.

This is how you say pteranodon:
teh-ran-oh-don

PTERANODON

Group: pterodactyloids

Wingspan: 29 feet (9 m)

Lived in: North America, Europe, Asia

When: Late Cretaceous, 120–65 million years ago

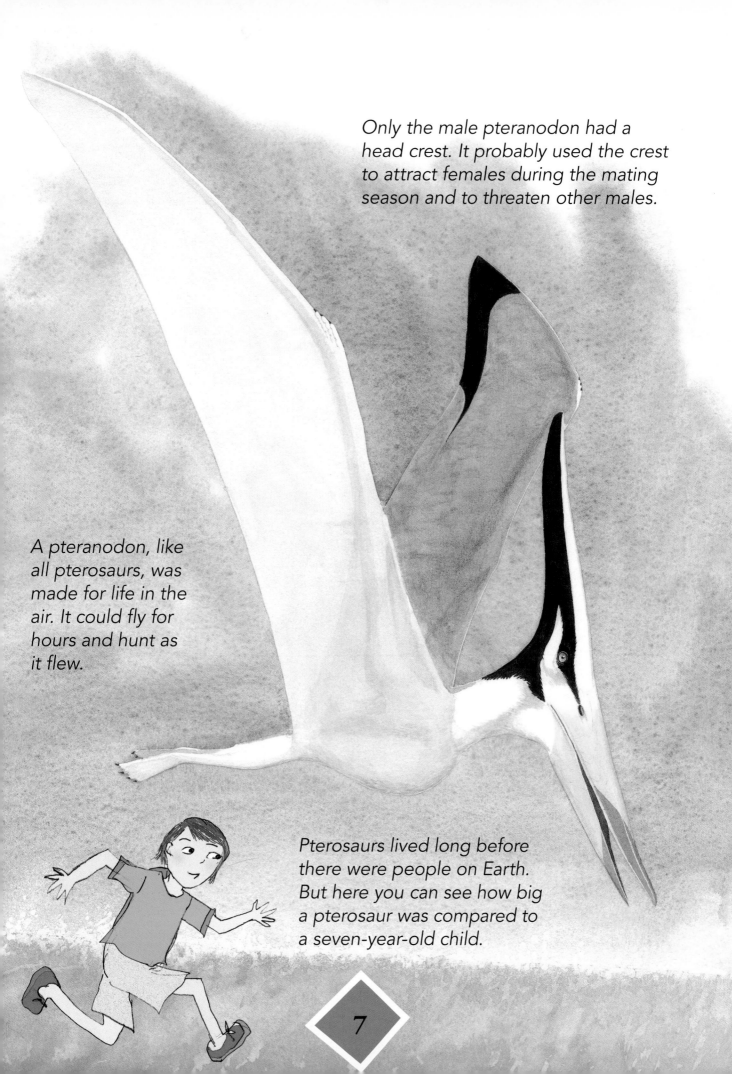

Only the male pteranodon had a head crest. It probably used the crest to attract females during the mating season and to threaten other males.

A pteranodon, like all pterosaurs, was made for life in the air. It could fly for hours and hunt as it flew.

Pterosaurs lived long before there were people on Earth. But here you can see how big a pterosaur was compared to a seven-year-old child.

Inside a pteranodon

The pteranodon's huge wings were made of tough, strong skin. The wings were attached to the bones of its arms and hands and to the sides of its body.

The fourth finger on each hand was extra long and held the top of the wing. The other three fingers were short and had sharp claws that the pterosaur used to walk or climb.

The pteranodon had large muscles on the breastbone and shoulders that helped it flap its gigantic wings and fly.

A pteranodon's bones were partly hollow and very light. This made it easier for the pteranodon to lift itself into the air.

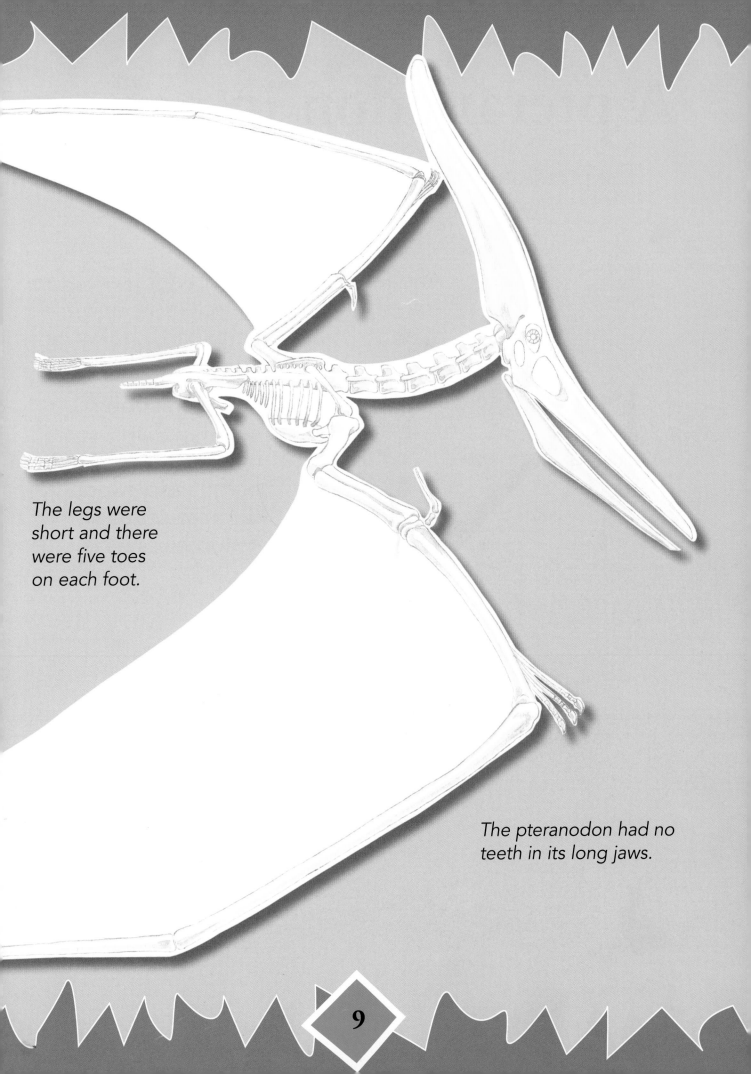

The legs were short and there were five toes on each foot.

The pteranodon had no teeth in its long jaws.

A pteranodon in action

The pterosaurs were the first vertebrates—animals with backbones—that could fly.

At one time, people thought pterosaurs could only glide, but scientists now think they were able to flap their wings and fly long distances.

The pteranodon could probably soar high above lakes and oceans and swoop down to seize fish in its toothless beak.

When it was walking, the pteranodon kept its long wings folded at its sides.

The pteranodon probably walked on all fours. It may have taken off into the air by running along the ground on two legs with its wings outstretched.

A pteranodon launches itself into the air from the edge of a cliff.

Eudimorphodon

So far, this is one of the earliest pterosaurs to be discovered. It was the largest of its time. It had a short neck and a long, bony tail that was about the same length as its body.

The eudimorphodon may have had to take off from a tree or a cliff because its long tail made it hard to run on land. It had a long beak and a lot of teeth that were unusual shapes. The teeth had several sharp points that probably helped the pterosaur hold on to slippery, wriggling fish.

12

EUDIMORPHODON

Group: rhamphorhynchoids

Wingspan: up to 3 feet (1 m)

Lived in: Europe

When: Late Triassic, 215–205 million years ago

This is how you say eudimorphodon: yoo-dee-morf-oh-don

The eudimorphodon probably hunted in the air. Or it might have perched on a branch over the water, ready to swoop when it saw a fish below.

13

Dimorphodon

A large head and bulky beak made this pterosaur look different from most of its relatives. Inside the beak were two very different types of teeth.

The dimorphodon had big, sharp fangs for catching prey, such as fish or squid, in the water. Behind these fangs were smaller, spiky teeth for holding on to a struggling catch.

The pterosaur also may have eaten shellfish and insects. The dimorphodon could climb trees using its clawed hands and rest there when it wasn't flying.

This is how you say dimorphodon:
die-morf-oh-don

The dimorphodon's beak might have been brightly colored, like a toucan's beak, to help it attract a mate.

DIMORPHODON

Group: rhamphorhynchoids

Wingspan: up to 3 feet (1 m)

Lived in: Europe

When: Early Jurassic, 200–180 million years ago

15

Rhamphorhynchus

This long-winged creature soared over seas and rivers like a giant seagull, searching for fish to eat.

The rhamphorhynchus probably swooped low to skim the water with the tip of its sharp lower jaw. It would snap up fish with the fangs that stuck out of its slender beak.

There was a flap of skin on the tip of the pterosaur's long tail. This might have helped it keep its balance in the air and steer.

RHAMPHORHYNCHUS

Group: rhamphorhynchoids

Wingspan: up to 5 feet (1.5 m)

Lived in: Europe and Africa

When: Late Jurassic, 170–144 million years ago

This is how you say rhamphorhynchus:
ram-for-ink-us

This pterosaur's body may have been covered with hair.

17

Sordes

The first fossils found of the sordes showed that the body of this little pterosaur was covered with hair! But most reptiles have scaly skin.

This may mean that other pterosaurs also had hairy coats and were warm-blooded, like birds and mammals are today. Most reptiles are cold-blooded and need to sit in the sun to warm up.

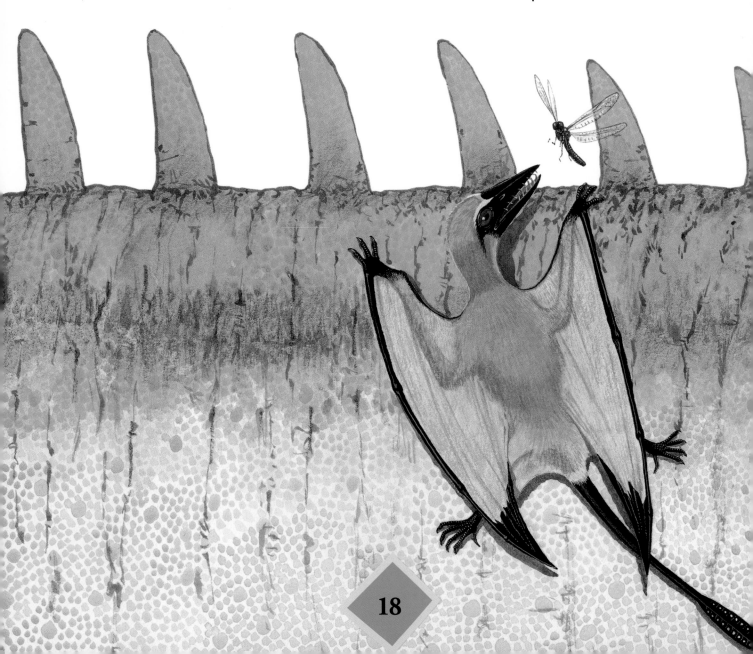

SORDES

Group: rhamphorhynchoids

Wingspan: 24 inches (60 cm)

Lived in: Asia

When: Late Jurassic, 180–144 million years ago

This is how you say sordes:
sor-deez

If the pterosaurs had been warm-blooded, they would have had plenty of energy to flap their wings and fly for long distances.

Pterodactylus

Pterodactyls had much shorter tails and longer necks than earlier pterosaurs. They also had larger brains, so they were probably expert hunters.

The pterodactylus laid eggs, like other pterosaurs. Pterosaurs probably kept their eggs warm and safe by burying them in sand or under a pile of plants.

When the young pterosaurs hatched, they looked like tiny versions of their parents, with jaws and wings. They had to fly and find their own food right away, with no help from their mom and dad.

PTERODACTYLUS

Group: pterodactyloids

Wingspan: up to 8 feet (2.5 m)

Lived in: Europe, Africa

When: Late Jurassic, 180–144 million years ago

This is how you say pterodactylus: ter-oh-dak-ti-lus

Young pterosaurs may have eaten different foods than their parents. For a small creature, insects and shellfish were easier to catch than fish.

Anhanguera

This giant pterosaur was bigger than the largest flying bird today—the wandering albatross.

The anhanguera was probably a strong flier and could soar for hours as it searched for fish. It had a large head that was almost twice the length of its small body. Its long jaws were lined with sharp teeth for catching fish.

When hunting, the anhanguera probably flew low over the water. It swooped down to scoop its prey from the sea.

ANHANGUERA

Group: pterodactyloids

Wingspan: up to 13 feet (4 m)

Lived in: South America

When: Early Cretaceous, 144–98 million years ago

This is how you say anhanguera:
an-yahn-gwer-a

Dsungaripterus and Pterodaustro

Both of these pterosaurs had unusual jaws that helped them eat their food.

Dsungaripterus had long, sharply pointed jaws that curved up at the tips. It may have used its jaws to pull shellfish from between rocks. Then it crushed the shells with the large flat teeth at the back of its jaws.

The dsungaripterus's beak worked both as a picker and a crusher.

DSUNGARIPTERUS

Group: pterodactyloids

Wingspan: up to 11 feet (3.5 m)

Lived in: Asia

When: Early Cretaceous, 144–98 million years ago

This is how you say dsungaripterus: jung-gah-rip-ter-us

The lower jaw of pterodaustro's beak was packed with up to 1,000 thin teeth that looked like the bristles in a toothbrush.

The pterosaur waded in the shallows, plunging its open beak into the water. When it lifted its head, small animals and plants were trapped on the bristles as the water drained out of the beak. The pterodaustro then swallowed its mouthful of food.

This is how you say pterodaustro:
ter-oh-dow-strow

The pterodaustro used its bristly jaw to strain small creatures from the water.

PTERODAUSTRO

Group: pterodactyloids

Wingspan: up to 6 feet (2 m)

Lived in: Brazil

When: Early Cretaceous, 144–98 million years ago

25

Quetzalcoatlus

This huge pterosaur was probably the biggest flying creature that has ever lived.

Its beak was longer than an adult human and its wings were three times as long as the wings of an albatross, the largest flying bird today.

The quetzalcoatlus was an expert flier and could probably glide for hours on its huge wings.

The quetzalcoatlus had a long neck and slender jaws. But it did not have teeth, and experts are not sure what it ate.

This is how you say quetzalcoatlus: ket-zal-koe-at-lus

This pterosaur may have been a scavenger that ate the bodies of dead dinosaurs. Or it might have used its long jaws to search in mud and shallow pools for shellfish and other small creatures.

QUETZALCOATLUS

Group: pterodactyloids

Wingspan: up to 39 feet (12 m)

Lived in: North America

When: Late Cretaceous, 98–65 million years ago

Other kinds of reptiles

Dinosaurs and pterosaurs were not the only reptiles living on Earth millions of years ago. There were also turtles, lizards, snakes, and crocodiles, and they all looked a lot like the reptiles we know today.

Two other groups of reptiles lived at the same time as the dinosaurs. These were the sea-living reptiles, such as plesiosaurs and ichthyosaurs, and the mammal-like reptiles. They all became extinct at the end of the Cretaceous period, 65 million years ago.

Plesiosaurs were large swimming reptiles with short tails and long flippers. They spent most of their time in the sea but laid their eggs on land, as turtles do today.

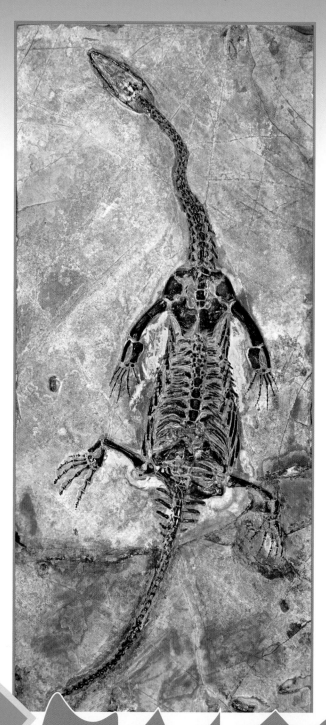

You can see the long neck and flippers on this fossilized skeleton of a plesiosaur. Plesiosaurs swam using their flippers.

Ichthyosaurs looked like dolphins. They never came onto land and gave birth to their young in the water. Both plesiosaurs and ichthyosaurs hunted other sea creatures, such as fish and squid.

Mammal-like reptiles were around before the dinosaurs. They were four-legged creatures that lived on land. Many of them looked more like mammals than reptiles and some may have been covered with hair. Mammals, including humans, may have evolved from mammal-like reptiles.

The cynognathus was a fierce mammal-like reptile. It had a strong, bulky body, a big head, and powerful jaws for killing its prey.

Words to know

Breastbone
The large bone in a bird's chest. A bird's wing muscles are attached to the breastbone.

Cold-blooded
A cold-blooded animal cannot control its own body heat. It sits in the sun to get warm or hides in the shade to cool down.

Crest
A bony shape on a pterosaur's head.

Fossils
Parts of an animal, such as bones and teeth, that have been preserved in rock over millions of years.

Predator
An animal that hunts and kills other animals.

Prey
Animals caught and killed by hunters such as the pteranodon.

Reptile
An animal with a backbone and a dry, scaly body. Most reptiles lay eggs with leathery shells. Dinosaurs were reptiles. Today's reptiles include lizards, snakes, turtles, and crocodiles.

Scavenger
An animal that eats creatures that are already dead.

Wandering albatross
The biggest flying bird today. The wings of a wandering albatross are more than 10 feet (3 m) from end to end.

Warm-blooded
A warm-blooded animal can control its body temperature, no matter how hot or cold the air is.

Index